THE ERUPTION OF VESUVIUS

The Deadly Disaster of Pompeii

Written by Mélanie Mettra
In collaboration with Damien Glad
Translated by Carly Probert

History 50MINUTES.com

THE ERUPTION OF VESUVIUS

KEY INFORMATION

- **When:** 24 August 79
- **Where:** Pompeii, Campania (Italy)
- **Context:**
  - Roman Empire
  - The eruption of Vesuvius
- **Main actors:**
  - Pliny the Elder, Latin naturalist and writer (23-79)
  - Pliny the Younger, Latin writer (61-114)
  - Giuseppe Fiorelli, Italian archaeologist (1823-1896)
- **Repercussions:**
  - A world-class archaeological site for the discovery of ancient life
  - Endangered remains

The city of Pompeii, located in the Italian Bay of Naples, is famous for the remarkable preservation of its remains and the exceptional testimony it provides of ancient life. Ironically, that which caused the disappearance of the city is also what protected it from the ravages of time. The eruption of Vesuvius on 24 August 79 indeed covered all the plains that lie between the slopes and the Mediterranean with a protective gangue, preserving it for over 1 500 years. However, although Pompeii is the symbol of this catastrophe, its inhabitants were not the only victims, and the land classified by UNESCO since 1997 exceeds the limits of this one city. There were actually five cities that were engulfed in the pyroclastic flow in this region of Campania:

Herculaneum, a maritime town of 5 000 inhabitants, the northernmost, Oplontis, a seaside city, Pompeii, the largest with about 20 000 inhabitants, Boscoreale, and finally to the south, the small port of Stabiae, where Pliny the Elder died on 25 August 79. Rediscovered in the 17th century, with the great advantage of being located in a very undeveloped area and therefore being accessible for excavations, there are now over 98 hectares that provide archaeologists, historians and visitors with an understanding of an intense life, but also the story of a terrible tragedy.

CONTEXT

POMPEII, AN ANCIENT CITY

Overview of Pompeii's ruins, engraving from *Die Gartenlaube*. Leipzig: Ernst Keil Edition, 1856.

When Vesuvius erupted, the plains surrounding it were populated. In fact, there were a total of four cities. The most active, from an economic and political point of view, was Pompeii. Totaling 20 000 inhabitants, it was located on a plateau at the mouth of the river Sarno. Its position allowed it to monitor the coast that extended from its feet. Oplontis was not strictly a town, but a residential and seaside neighborhood of Pompeii. Herculaneum, further north, was a port that accommodated both luxurious residences and fishermen's houses. Stabiae was a wealthy seaside resort.

The hinterland had numerous villas, and agricultural land extended almost to the top of Vesuvius.

Settlement in this territory was ancient. Despite the risks from volcanic areas, the particular fertility of the soil there was attractive. Although remains from the end of prehistory have been found in Pompeii, the first installation of a real village seems to date back to the 7th century B.C., with the installation of Oscan people (people that came from the Apennines). First under Greek influence, Pompeii then passed to the Etruscans who gained the south of Italy from Tuscany during the 6th century B.C., founding new cities as they went. The city's position was strategic for the Etruscans, who faced the powerful Greek colonies. Indeed, the site allowed for both control of the sea and of the fertile valley of the Sarno, a navigable river that leads to another Etruscan city, Nucera, thus connecting the Mediterranean maritime trade with the interior of Campania. Therefore, the Etruscans seem to have united the local people in organized cities.

However, in the 5th century B.C., first the Greeks, after the naval victory of Cuma (474 B.C.), then the Samnites arrived in Campania from the Appenines, undermining the Etruscan civilization. The Samnites then took possession of Pompeii. The city spread, surrounded by impressive fortifications, and the countryside was organized into farms. But the Romans, whose power began to exceed the Latium (central Italian region), became formidable opponents. During the second war between the Romans and the Samnites, at the end of the 4th century B.C. (327-302), the Samnites were forced to hand over control of Campania to their opponents. The Samnite Pompeii became the ally of Rome and remained its ally during the second Punic War (218-201 B.C.), against the Carthaginian Hannibal (general and statesman, 247-183 B.C.). This loyalty enabled it to thrive throughout the 3rd and 2nd centuries B.C. The city was growing, both within its fortifications and across its territory, where agricultural properties thrived. But in 90 B.C., the social war (from *socii*, Latin, meaning "allies") between Rome and its allied cities broke out.

THE SOCIAL WAR: ROME'S CONQUEST OF ITALY

At the dawn of our era, Italy was composed of a mosaic of peoples (Samnites, Marsi, Apulians, Lucanians, Gauls, etc.), whose cities had, over the years of conflicts and defeats, allied with Rome. But in the early 1st century B.C., tensions were rising. Indeed, while using the armed forces supplied by allies to conquer new territories, Rome still considered these allies to be its vassals and did not hesitate to interfere in their political and economic life. When a bill was established aiming to allow only Roman citizens to benefit from public land obtained by the Romans during their conquests, the tribune Livius Drusus (died in 91 B.C.) was against this idea and advocated the granting of Roman citizenship to all inhabitants of allied cities before the Senate. The refusal of this idea, as well as his assassination, added fuel to the fire.

The allied cities then tried to meet in a confederation (the "Italic confederation", after the name of the peoples of the peninsula), under the direction of the Marsi Quintus Pompedius Silo (died 88 B.C.) and Samnite Claudius Papius Mutilis. In 90 B.C., under Julian law, Rome finally agreed to extend Roman citizenship to all the cities which did not rebel against its authority.

ROMAN CITIZENSHIP

In the 1st century, Roman citizenship applied to five categories of men:

- The sons of a Roman citizen;
- The freed slaves of Roman citizens;
- Foreigners who had served in the Roman army for more than 24 years;
- Magistrates of foreign cities governed by Latin law;
- The inhabitants of any city conquered by favor of the emperor.

However, only the citizen sons of Roman citizens could access the magistracy and the Senate.

After the social war, the allied cities of southern Italy and Cisalpine Gaul and Gaul (edict of Emperor Claudius, 48) obtained citizenship for their inhabitants, provided they meet the financial criteria. Finally, the Edict of Caracalla (212) granted citizenship to all free men of the empire.

Once acquired, it gave access to civil, political and military rights, and allowed in particular for the following of the *cursus honorum*, which gave access to the highest administrative positions in Rome. It was also accompanied by obligations such a tax payment, identification, financial or personal involvement in the defense of the empire, etc.

At the same time, Rome sent its armies, led by General Sulla (138-78 B.C.), to subdue the rebels, which included Herculaneum and Pompeii. The first became a *municipium* (cited autonomous government, often modeled on Roman institutions, with a reduced right of citizenship), while the second was proclaimed a Roman colony in 80 B.C., under the name of Colonia Cornelia Veneria Pompeianorum ("colony dedicated to Venus Pompeiana"). The colony differed from the *municipium* in the sense that half of its population were settlers (Roman citizens) and half were from the indigenous Italics. Many Romans then moved to Pompeii, occupying the residences of former elites and Samnites whose land holdings had been appropriated.

This was followed by an era of prosperity, which continued under the empire. Under the reign of Augustus (Roman emperor, 63-14 B.C.), Campania was attached to Lazio to constitute the first administrative region of the Roman Empire. Augustus favored the bourgeoisie of Pompeii, including old local families, in order to attract their support. In return, they helped to enrich the city, celebrating the imperial cult, which was public and compulsory, through magnificent architectural achievements. Under his reign, aqueducts and water towers were also built, which supplied water to not only public fountains, but also the private houses of

Herculaneum and Pompeii. Prosperity continued with the successors of Augustus. The cities of the Neapolitan bay attracted the Roman aristocracy, who moved to the city, but especially to the villas of the countryside and the seaside.

But Pompeii was not only a resort. It was primarily a leading merchant city, characterized by the intensity of its trade with the rest of the empire. It attracted a cosmopolitan population and enjoyed a lively political life. With the eruption of 24 August, this vitality would come to an abrupt end.

DID YOU KNOW?

The cities of Pompeii and the Bay of Naples attracted many Roman personalities. Two of them in particular left evidence of their taste for their Campanian residences. Poppea (30-65), the second wife of Emperor Nero (37-68) had a residence in Oplontis, whose remains are still visible today and attest to its refinement. Cicero (Roman philosopher and politician, 106-43 B.C.) also stayed regularly at his villa in Pompeii, where he composed some of his writings, and which he praised for its charms in his correspondence. Spartacus (Thracian gladiator slave, died in 71 B.C.), head of the slave revolt in 73 B.C., found refuge on the slopes of Vesuvius before fleeing to Gaul.

THE ERUPTION OF VESUVIUS

Representations of the volcano, beneath which lay these prosperous cities, show a sharp mountain peak covered with cultivated land, particularly vineyards. The first Greek settlers in the area had nicknamed it "Campi Flegrei" ("burning fields"), in reference to the boiling water resurgences. Some authors, such as Strabo (Greek geographer, c. 64 B.C.-25 A.D.), described the volcanic nature of the terrain. The tranquility that reigned for several hundred years made the inhabitants forget about the danger of the location. The first warning shot took place on 5 February 62. The stories of Tacitus (Roman historian, 56-117) in the *Annales* and Seneca (Roman philosopher, politician and playwright, 4 B.C.-65 A.D.) in *Questioni Naturali*, and a marble bas-relief found in a villa in Pompeii all attest to an earthquake (estimated magnitude of 5), with Pompeii at the epicenter and which destroyed much of the city. When, in 79, Vesuvius awoke and erupted, the city was still being reconstructed.

BIOGRAPHIES

Pliny the Elder.

Born in 23, probably in Como, Pliny the Elder was a Latin writer from a wealthy family of the equestrian order. He studied at the school of rhetoricians of Rome, then became a cavalry officer in Germany between 47 and 57. He inter-rupted his military career during the reign of Nero, when he resided mainly in Rome.

Appointed Attorney of Narbonne (Roman province of southern Gaul) and Hispania by the successor of Nero, Vespasian (9-79), he took to the road and traveled to North Africa. Recalled to Rome to the Emperor's side to be his personal adviser, he was appointed commander of the fleet stationed at Misenum on the Emperor's death, north of the Bay of Naples, by the new Emperor Titus (38-81). Witnessing the eruption of Vesuvius in 79, he chartered a ship to observe it more closely and to rescue his friends from Stabiae, where he died of asphyxiation.

Passionate about learning and motivated by an insatiable curiosity, he wrote many works throughout his life in the fields of science, military history, imperial history – conti-nuing the work of Livy (Roman historian, 59 B.C.-17 A.D.) – grammar and rhetoric, and especially *A Natural History* in 37 books, dedicated to Titus. This summary of ancient zoological, botanical and geographical knowledge is the only work to have reached us.

PLINY THE YOUNGER, LATIN WRITER

Born in Como in 61, fatherless and raised by his guardians, Verginius Rufus (14-97), victor of the uprising of the Roman province of Lyon, senator, governor of Cisalpine Gaul and Roman consul under Emperor Nerva (30-98), and Pliny the Elder, his uncle, who adopted him in his will. He studied in Rome, in particular receiving the teachings of the famous rhetorician Quintilian (35-100). A successful lawyer, he followed the traditional *curriculum honorum* to access the Senator position. He was appointed imperial legate of Bithynia by Trajan (Roman Emperor, 53-117) in 111.

His correspondence with his literary friends and with the Emperor Trajan was a masterful literary work and a precious testimony on the life and thinking of this century. It was in his letters to his friend Tacitus that he tells the story of the death of his uncle during the eruption of Vesuvius, providing a unique description of the event.

He died in 113.

A FAMOUS DESCRIPTION

The detailed description of the eruption of Vesuvius in 79 by Pliny the Younger passed to posteriry in archaeology and history, but also in volcanology. Indeed, the word "Plinian" refers to a type of eruption characterized by a viscous magma, the rise of which triggers violent explosions resulting in the issuance of eruptive clouds of several kilometers in height, followed by falling ash and volcanic fragments, based on the model of Vesuvius.

GIUSEPPE FIORELLI, ITALIAN ARCHAEOLOGIST

Born in Naples on 8 June 1823, Giuseppe Fiorelli studied archeology and numismatics. A member of the Archaeological Museum in Naples, he carried out his first excavations at Pompeii in 1848 for the museums. He returned to the site in 1860, this time on behalf of the University of Naples, where he was a professor of archaeology.

He was the first to implement a search technique respecting the different archaeological strata. He also proceeded to disengage the streets, which were often neglected and cluttered with the rubble resulting from clearing the houses. He installed order in the city, which was gradually divided into regions and districts (*insulae*) and gave a number to each dwelling. The same careful attention was applied to the objects that he found. These were identified, numbered and listed in specific search books, published under the title *Historia Pompeianorum Antiquitatum*. However, his most famous achievement was the molding of some victims of the eruption. Indeed, the ashes, once solidified, retained the imprint of what they have covered, particularly the bodies, human and animal, of the victims of the disaster. The decomposition of organic matter gad created an empty space in the ask pocket. Guiseppe Fiorelli poured plaster in the pocket, before breaking the shell of hardened ash. He thus obtained body casts, frozen in the position where death had seized them. This process would then be applied to trace decomposed elements (food scraps, wood elements, etc.).

Appointed Director of the Naples National Museum and director of the Italian National Antiquities in 1875, he died in Naples on 28 January 1896.

THE DEATH AND REBIRTH OF POMPEII

24 AUGUST 79

"On 24 August, in the early afternoon, my mother drew his attention to a cloud of unusual size and appearance. [...] It was not clear at that distance from which mountain the cloud was rising (it was afterwards known to be Vesuvius); [...] In places it looked white, elsewhere blotched and dirty, according to the amount of soil and ashes it carried with it. [...] Ashes were already falling, hotter and thicker as the ships drew near, followed by bits of pumice and blackened stones, charred and cracked by the flames [...] Meanwhile on Mount Vesuvius broad sheets of fire and leaping flames blazed at several points, their bright glare emphasized by the darkness of night.

For several days past there had been earth tremors which were not particularly alarming because they are frequent in Campania: but that night the shocks were so violent that everything felt as if it were not only shaken but overturned [...] at any rate it receded from the shore so that quantities of sea creatures were left stranded on dry sand. On the landward side a fearful black cloud was rent by forked and quivering bursts of flame, and parted to reveal great tongues of fire, like flashes of lightning magnified in size [...] A gleam of light returned, but we took this to be a warning of the approaching flames rather than daylight."

(Extracts from the letters of Pliny the Younger to Tacitus telling of the death of Pliny the Elder)

These extracts of the letters of Pliny the Younger to his friend Tacitus tell the woeful story of Campania in August

79. The eruption began a few days before, with a series of earthquakes and the disappearance of springs. On the night of 23-24, the first explosion, which was only light, brought fine dust and some debris from the crater. This was probably noticed only by the inhabitants of the villas that occupied the slopes of Vesuvius. It was one of them, Rectina, the wife of a friend of Pliny the Elder, who decided to send him a call for help to Misenum. In the afternoon of 24 August, a shower of ash and pumice fell on the Bay of Naples, and the cloud that contained it plunged them into total darkness.

The eruption of Vesuvius 24 August 79, by Pierre-Henri de Valenciennes, 1813.

Throughout the day, the size of stones increased and destroyed the roofs of houses, which had already been weakened by earthquakes. The sea was also agitated by the telluric movement and began to withdraw, a sign of the tsunami that would strike the coast a few hours later. On 25 August, pyroclastic flows succeeded the shower of ash, a mass of material and gas of over 400 degrees, rushing down the slopes of the volcano at speeds of up to 600 km per hour and burning everything in their path. Pompeii was buried first, followed by Herculaneum, which was also covered in mud pushed by an outpouring of magma coming from the collapsed crater.

Part of the population, terrified, tried to shut themselves in their homes, which, under the weight of debris raining down, collapsed. The inhabitants of Pompeii that remained in the streets were suffocated by the burning gases and their bodies were trapped in a cast of ash. Others who attempted to escape by sea perished in the tidal wave. Many, however, managed to escape the cataclysm by leaving the city on foot or by chariot.

Molding of a victim of the eruption buried in a sitting position

A CONTROVERSIAL DATE

Although the date of the eruption is known to us through the letter of Pliny the Younger to Tacitus, it is now the subject of much controversy. There is doubt as to what Pliny really wrote, as well as its transcription, as the phrase used to indicate the date was not common in Latin syntax. Moreover, archaeological research suggests that the event took place in autumn, as victims were found wearing clothing that was too thick for August. In addition, braziers seem to have been lit, indicating a certain freshness. Other indications, such as fruit and vegetables, the study of wind conditions and the direction of the cloud of ash tend to confirm that the eruption occurred in October.

THE AFTERMATH OF THE CATASTROPHE

In two days, Vesuvius had claimed a considerable number of victims. At Pompeii, it was an estimated 10% of the population (2 000 people, out of a population of approximately 20 000 inhabitants) and, in the region, a total of between 10 000 and 20 000 deaths. The landscape was apocalyptic. However, the stupor was short-lived and the city of Pompeii, which was only covered in two to three meters of volcanic debris (compared to twenty in Herculaneum) soon saw the arrival of both its residents who had fled and looters, looking for abandoned treasures in the destroyed houses. But the Emperor Titus had the rubble guarded. Gradually, nobody was interested in the field of ruins anymore when nature asserted its rights once again. The place was renamed Civita (meaning "city"), until its rediscovery and identification in the 18th century.

THE REBIRTH OF POMPEII

Until the late 16th century, the buried cities were covered with vineyards and crops. Between 1592 and 1600, the construction of a canal on the Sarno River by Italian architect Domenico Fontana (1543-1607) brought paintings, coins and inscriptions to the surface, but the engineer had them covered up. Undoubtedly, throughout the centuries many remains have appeared during well drilling and field plowing, all random finds which were unattractive to their contemporaries.

However, in the 18th century, during the reign of Charles VII (King of Naples from 1716 to 1788), archaeology, and especially the discovery of ancient art objects began to take a certain prestige. When he heard of the discoveries made at Herculaneum in 1738, the sovereign launched excavations conducted by the engineer Roque Joachim de Alcubierre (1702-1780). In 1748, it was the site of Pompeii's turn to be excavated by the abbot Martorelli, and in 1763 the city was identified.

These excavations were disorderly, as their purpose was to collect works of art, not to study ancient civilization. Anything that did not seem to have an aesthetic value was destroyed and the premises were filled once again after being explored. These practices, denounced by the man considered to be the first art historian and a specialist in ancient times, Johann Joachim Winckelmann (1717-1768), also served to promote the reputation of the two sites that attracted prestigious guests.

This frenzy continued under Napoleonic rule, encouraged by Joachim Murat (Marshal of France and King of Naples, 1767-1815) and his wife Caroline Bonaparte (1782-1839). After a quieter period following the fall of the French princes, the beginning of the period of the unification of Italy (1815-1870) and the brief passage of Alexandre Dumas (French man of letters, 1802-1870) appointed by Giuseppe Garibaldi (Italian politician, 1807-1882) as Superintendent of excavations, King Victor-Emmanuel II of Italy (1820-1878) entrusted the management of the site to archaeologist Giuseppe Fiorelli. Excavations were now of a scientific nature.

In 1875, his successor, Michele Ruggiero, launched the first major restoration and consolidation of frescoes. The passion and intensity of the excavations and restorations did not stop in the 20th century, led this time by Vittorio Spinazzola (1863-1943) and Amadeo Maiuri (1886-1963). The site, which included the cities of Herculaneum, Pompeii and the current Torre Annunziata, near the site of Stabiae, was declared a World Heritage Site by UNESCO in 1997. In recent decades, the problem no longer lies in the excavations, but in the preservation of this heritage, which is now deteriorating rapidly after being protected for over 1700 years.

DID YOU KNOW?

After having being renowned in Roman times, the sites of Herculaneum and Pompeii became precious to the European princes and intellectuals of the 18th century. For the Emperor Joseph II of Habsburg (1741-1790) in 1771, the German poet Goethe (1749-1832) in 1787, the

French writers Chateaubriand (1768-1848) in 1804, Théophile Gautier (1811-1872) in 1830, Stendhal (1783-1842) and Nerval (1808-1855), Pompeii was an essential landmark, a symbol both to promote the Italian government and inspire poets.

Paradoxically, the disappearance of Pompeii allowed for its entry into eternity.

HERITAGE THREATENED ONCE AGAIN

The fate of the remains brought to light is not always positive. Indeed, the discovery means that the ruins are subject to changes due to contact with air, dryness, moisture, light, and especially with the public. Although objects can benefit from specific conservation measures, these measures are more complicated to implement when it comes to monuments and the sites of Vesuvius are not immune to these problems. Although Pompeii suffered bombings during World War II (1939-1945), an earthquake in 1980, the onslaught of bad weather and the annual attendance of nearly 2 million visitors, it is now financial problems that weaken it. With the economic crises in the peninsula and the whole of Europe, the budget allocated to culture in Italy had been reduced and it can no longer pay for projects to restore and preserve the site, nor the maintenance and caretaking. The paintings and mosaics are degrading, the frescoes are peeling away, buildings are collapsing, both in places rarely visited by tourists and in the most visited neighborhoods. The collapse of the house of gladiators, in November 2010, however, alerted the public and UNESCO sounded the alarm. The EU then called upon Italy to use the funds made available to the government for restoration projects before 2015, or they would have to repay the sums that had been given to them. However, administrative delays and the attribution problems with restoration markets leave the city of Pompeii with little hope.

THE ARCHAEOLOGICAL SITE AND DISCOVERIES

The current neglect suffered by the ancient Gulf cities poses a threat to the invaluable heritage. The eruption of 79 had suddenly frozen, and more importantly protected, in an extraordinary and unique way, places that had been caught in their full vitality. Herculaneum, Pompeii and Stabiae therefore provide incredible testimonies of ancient life down to the tiniest of details. One can follow the evolution of the habitat, customs, trade and political life over five centuries.

HABITAT

The excavations have unveiled different times of the Pompeian habitat. The oldest traces reveal houses organized into blocks around a loosely organized street network, within the walls of the tuff fortifications (local volcanic rock). The middle class lived in kind of subdivisions where the houses were almost identical: they were composed of a corridor leading to two rooms, at the end of which was a living room, followed by a series of rooms in the back and a small vegetable garden. During the Samnite period (5th-1st centuries B.C.), the elites had *atrium* houses: the living room became a reception room, marked by a central opening overlooking a pond.

In the 2nd century B.C., the opulence of the city and its close links with the Greek cities that surrounded the Mediterranean and those with whom they traded, led to the construction of luxurious residences. Double *atrium* houses (one private and one for reception) increased, the utility garden became a pleasure garden, transformed into a peristyle (surrounded by columns and shaded roofs) under Hellenistic influence, also visible in the decoration. There were floor mosaics in the wealthiest houses (some were nearly 3 000 m²), representing scenes from Greek history. The mosaic also suggests scenes of everyday life, such as the famous *cave canem* that warned passersby of the presence of a dog. The murals of the Samnite era, which served to mask masonry, imitated marble. Ordinary houses did not have floors covered with mosaics, but were mainly made of bare ground or tuff cobblestone.

After obtaining the status of a Roman colony, homes continued to evolve, spreading beyond the city walls, which had become obsolete. Many recreational and vacation homes settled on the shores of the Gulf of Naples, such as the Villa of Mysteries or the Villa of Diomedes, near Herculaneum. The townhouse, in a city whose plan was Romanized, with straight and perpendicular streets set around a cardo (lane running through the center of the city from north to south), opened wide onto the outside with terraces. The décor also changed: paintings became optical illusions, creating new virtual spaces such as gardens or animated theatrical scenes of life-size figures. Later, painting became symbolic, mirroring an imaginary fed by mythology and exoticism, while mosaics experimented with polychromy and geometry.

The dense Pompeian economic activity and the diversity of populations that coexisted in Pompeii (old Samnite families, rich Roman colonists, but also a bourgeoisie of Campanian or foreign merchants) influenced domestic architecture from Roman times. The bourgeois mansions, unlike the aristocratic houses, lacked state rooms and reception rooms, but sometimes spread over an impressive surface. They often added an entire floor, either to accommodate the apartments of servants and slaves, or to be rented out, as was more usually the case in the homes of the middle classes. Notably, the city was not divided into districts based on social foundations: a bourgeois residence could adjoin both a palace and a more modest house.

ECONOMIC LIFE

Numerous buildings reflect the vibrant economy of Pompeii. The *tabernae* (places dedicated to selling), such as the *Taberna Fortunatae*, lined the streets, which were mostly paved, providing inhabitants with fruits, vegetables, cereals, wine, but also handicrafts, fabrics and jewelry. Graffiti found on the walls of these *tabernae* allows us to learn price of wine: 1 ace for a low-quality wine, 4 for Falernian wine, the great vintage of its time.

There were also bakeries, whose business is described in frescoes and mosaics. The *thermopolia*, stalls where the poorest people could eat on the go during the day, such as the Laraire *thermopolium*, with marble countertops in which *dolia* were embedded, huge jars filled with food, to allow residents and visiting traders to have their meals. The contents of these *dolia* (olives, fish in brine, dried and boiled vegetables, etc.) have occasionally been found, providing an extraordinary testimony of the food of the Pompeians.

Thermopolium of Lucius Vetutius Placidus in the city of Pompeii.

The *macellum* also symbolizes the commercial importance of Pompeii. The food market had a place specifically dedicated to it. In addition to a line of shops and essential *sacellum* (place dedicated to the imperial cult), street vendors set up their stalls in places that they had previously reserved at the municipality. The sellers of fresh products had a fountain where they could keep their goods, and a table of weights to ensure the honesty of the sellers. Dyers, tanneries, and even brothels were as richly decorated with friezes and murals as the houses, allowing us to get a glimpse of the active daily life of the city.

POLITICAL AND RELIGIOUS LIFE

The political and religious life of Pompeii is known first of all thanks to the usual public buildings that characterized the life of every Roman city: forum, basilicas and temples were scattered throughout the city. They also illustrate the evolution of architecture and its influences. The Temple of Apollo, the oldest, was installed by the Etruscans, while the Temple of Isis, dating back to the 2nd century B.C., represents the Samnite design of public architecture. The Temple of Jupiter, from roughly the same time, was converted into a capitol with the Roman colonization of the city, showing the adaptation and reuse of buildings at the whim of successive influences.

The elites of the imperial period, to attract the votes of their fellow citizens in the elections, but also to show their power and consolidate their image, competed in the spending of their private funds to beautify the city, enlarging the ancient monuments, replacing tuff with marble and building new facilities dedicated to public life, particularly leisure.

LEISURE AND DAILY LIFE

The prosperity of Pompeii is also reflected in its recreational facilities. The city had two thermal facilities, which date back to the 1st century B.C., an amphitheater, a theater and an *odeon* (place dedicated to musical performances), a *palaestra* (place of athletic training with a swimming pool). The water supply, which dates back to the Samnite installation, greatly improved over the centuries with the construction of aqueducts that filled the water towers (14 were found, spread throughout the city), thus providing the city of Pompeii with running waters thanks to kilometers of lead piping. The houses, gardens, and especially the public fountains installed on every street corner, and the thermal baths benefitted from these facilities.

In addition, the ash preserved what would normally disappear quickly: organic matter. Along with the human and animals remains that were found, others were surprised by the fiery clouds and frozen in the moment: dogs trying to escape from their chain, mules trying to flee the walls of the bakery where they were operating the wheel. Food leftovers such as bread, *dolia* contents, olives and nut shells complete the picture of the life of the city, captured alive by the anger of the volcano.

Did you know?

The richness of Pompeian discoveries is also based on rare discoveries whose quantity is valuable. Indeed, because of the state of conservation of buildings and walls, many pieces of graffiti were found, often humorous, virulent, spontaneous and poetic, but also sometimes vulgar. Many buildings were thus identified through the inscriptions engraved there. They also provided information on prices of food, wine, and entry to the thermal baths. We can still find inscriptions made during the elections, but also invectives left by individuals. Far from being simple phrases written on stone, the graffiti of Pompeii is a symbol of the extraordinary breath of fresh air that ran through the city.

SUMMARY

- The city of Pompeii was founded in the 6th century B.C., in the Gulf of Naples, near Mount Vesuvius.
- It became a Roman colony in approximately 80 B.C.
- Partly destroyed by an earthquake in 62 and rebuilt, it was buried under a shower of ash following the eruption of Vesuvius on 24 August 79, the story of which has been passed down to us through the letters of Pliny the Younger.
- Having been totally forgotten, the first traces of the city found were reported in the late 16th century and the first excavations took place in 1748.
- These excavations were pursued by Napoleon Bonaparte and Joachim Murat, when they possessed the Kingdom of Naples, but did not become systematic until 1860, particularly under the direction of archaeologist Giovanni Fiorelli.
- The site of Pompeii, Herculaneum and Torre Annunziata (Oplontis), representing an area of 98 hectares, has been classified as a World Heritage Site of UNESCO since 1997.
- The site is now in danger from lack of maintenance due to the mismanagement of funds.

FIND OUT MORE

BIBLIOGRAPHY

- Barbet, A. (2001) *Les cités enfouies du Vésuve. Pompéi, Herculanum, Baies, Stabies*. Paris: Fayard.
- Coarelli, F. (2005) *Pompéi, la vie ensevelie*. Paris: Larousse.
- Etienne, R. (1998) *La vie quotidienne à Pompéi*. Paris: Hachette.
- Géroudet, N. (2005) La représentation figurée du tremblement de terre romain de 62 apr. J.-C. à Pompéi : médiatisation d'une catastrophe naturelle ? In Lavier, R. and Granet-Abisset, A.-M. (eds.) *Récits et représentations des catastrophes depuis l'Antiquité*. Grenoble, CNRS-MSH Alps.
- Grimal, P. (1963) *The Civilisation of Rome*. Crow's Nest (Australia): Allen & Unwin.
- Lamoine, L. (2009) *Le pouvoir local en Gaule romaine*. Clermont-Ferrand: Presses Universitaires Blaise-Pascal.
- Lessing, E. and Varone, A. (1996) *Pompeii*. Paris, Éditions du Terrail.
- Robert-Boissier, B. (2011) *Pompéi. Les doubles vies de la cité du Vésuve*. Paris: Ellipses.
- Van Andringa W. (2013) *Pompéi: mythologie et histoire*. Paris: Éditions du CNRS.

ADDITIONAL SOURCES

- Beard, M. (2010) *Pompeii: The Life of a Roman Town*. London: Profile Books.
- Pompeiisites.org (No date) *History*. [Online].

[Accessed 9 December 2016]. Available from:
<http://www.pompeiisites.org/Sezione.
jsp?titolo=HISTORY&idSezione=6784>
* Scarth, A. (2009) *Vesuvius: A Biography*. New Jersey:
Princeton University Press.

SOURCES ICONOGRAPHIQUES

* Overview of Pompeii's ruins, engraving from *Die
Gartenlaube*. Leipzig: Ernst Keil Edition, 1856. Royalty-
free reproduction picture.
* Pliny the Elder. © Cesare Cantù, *Grande Illustrazione
del Lombardo Veneto. Ossia storia delle città, dei borghi,
comuni, castelli ecc.*, Volume III. Milan: Corona e Caimi,
1859.
* *Vesuvius Eruption the 24 August 79* by Pierre-Herri de
Valenciennes, 1813. Royalty-free reproduction picture.
* Molding of a victim of the eruption buried in a sitting
position. © Jebulon.
* Thermopolium of Lucius Vetutius Placidus in the city of
Pompeii. © Daniele Florio.

NOVELS

* Bulwer-Lytton, E. (2016) *The Last Days of Pompeii*.
CreateSpace Independent Publishing Platform.
* Gautier, T. (2016) *Arria Marcella: A Souvenir of Pompeii*.
Trans. Sumichrast, F.C. Schooner & Co Publishing.
* Harris, R. (2009) *Pompeii*. New York: Ballantine Books.

FILMS AND DOCUMENTARIES

- *The Last Days of Pompeii.* (1959) [Film]. Mario Bonnard and Sergio Leone. Dir. Italy: Cine-Produzioni Associate, Procusa, Transocean-Film.
- *Out of the Ashes: Recovering the Lost Library of Herculaneum.* (2003) [Documentary]. Julie Walker. Dir. USA.
- *The Lost City of Pompeii.* (2013) [Documentary]. Chris Holt. Dir. UK.

IMPROVE YOUR GENERAL KNOWLEDGE

IN A BLINK OF AN EYE !

www.50minutes.com